DOVE

INCLUDES ASHBOURNE AND SURROUNDING VILLAGES

PRINCESS OF RIVERS

Dovedale is without doubt the best known and most loved of all the dales of the White Peak. With over two million visitors every year, it is the top of almost everyone's "must see" list when they visit the Peak District, Britain's first and most popular national park.

The River Dove – the name comes from the Celtic *dubh* and means "the dark river" – forms the border between Derbyshire and Staffordshire. It rises on the moorland of Axe Edge west of Buxton, a place marked by a slab inscribed by the initials of Izaak Walton and Charles Cotton – the dale's first and finest publicists.

The growing river flows south past the villages of Hollinsclough, Crowdecote and Hartington and enters Beresford Dale, Wolfscote Dale and Mill Dale, before the dale finally takes the name of its river at the hamlet of Milldale. After the scenic splendours of Dovedale itself, the river flows on to the south through Rocester and Tutbury, to eventually meet the mighty River Trent at Newton Solney, near Repton.

ABOVE: Thorpe Cloud and the Stepping Stones crossing the River Dove

HISTORY OF THE DALE

Charles Cotton, the spendthrift squire of Beresford Hall in the upper reaches of the Dove, knew the river like the back of his hand, having been born and raised within a stones throw of its banks.

So he made the perfect guide (going under the name of Viator) to Izaak Walton (who is known as Piscator) in their classic fisherman's bible, *The Compleat Angler*. This was one of the most successful works in the English language, first published in 1653 and never out of print since.

Cotton often hid from his many creditors in Dovedale's caves, such as Reynard's and Frank i' th Rocks Cave in Wolfscote Dale. But when he was not avoiding his creditors, Cotton was almost single-handedly putting Dovedale and the Peak District on the tourist map. Apart from the best-selling *Complete Angler*, his 1681 version of *The Wonders of the Peake* – a rehashing of Thomas Hobbes' original – was one of the earliest popular guidebooks to the region.

Lord Byron, of Newstead Abbey, Nottinghamshire, writing to his friend the Irish poet Tom Moore, famously claimed: "Was you ever in Dovedale? I can assure you there are things in Derbyshire as noble as Greece or Switzerland." Moore, the author of *Lalla Rookh*, followed his friend's recommendation and came to live at Mayfield, near Ashbourne in 1813.

LEFT: Izaak Walton RIGHT: Fly fishing on the River Dove

But in the event, Byron never visited him there, complaining when Moore left: "I don't know whether to be glad or sorry that you are leaving Mayfield. Had I been at Newstead during your stay there... we should have been within hail, and I should like to have made a giro (circuit) of the Peak with you. I know that country well, having been all over it when a boy."

People have been flooding to see the wonders of Dovedale, the best-known and loved of all the Peakland dales, ever since. As John Ruskin, the Victorian conservationist and critic observed, describing Derbyshire: "The whole glory of the country is in its glens. The wide acreage of field or moor above is wholly without interest; it is only in the clefts of it, and the dingles, that the traveller finds his joy."

Dovedale became even more accessible to visitors when the Ashbourne-Buxton railway line reached Thorpe Cloud station, near the village of Thorpe, in 1899. The line closed in 1968 and was converted into the walkers' and cyclists' track known as the Tissington Trail, which opened in 1971.

About two million people still 'find their joy' in Dovedale, which is now in the ownership of the National Trust. The main part of the dale was acquired by the Trust in 1934 after years of vigorous campaigning by Mr FA Holmes of Buxton, who is commemorated by a plaque near Lion's Head Rock, and the gift of industrialist Sir Robert McDougall of Manchester. Successive areas were gradually added to the Trust's ownership until 1938, and finally, Wolfscote Dale became part of what is now the Trust's Peak District Estate in 1948.

In the 1930s, Dovedale was even proposed in Parliament as a separate National Park, and it eventually became part of the Peak District National Park when it was designated in April, 1951.

A comprehensive 10-year programme of restoration on the five-mile-long footpath through the dale between the Stepping Stones and Wolfscote Dale was completed in 1992 by the National Park Authority, the National Trust, Derbyshire and Staffordshire County Councils, and Severn Trent Water at a cost of £¼ million.

Dovedale became a National Nature Reserve in 2006 in recognition of its place as "one of England's finest wildlife sites," with its diverse flora and fauna, and fascinating geology.

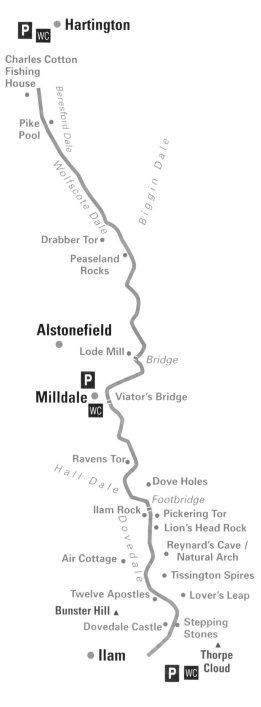

TOP: Beresford Dale
MIDDLE: View from Air Cottage
BOTTOM: Tissington Spires

GEOLOGY: THE STORY OF THE ROCKS

Dovedale is a classic example of what geologists call an "incised meander", where the modern, apparently insignificant River Dove, which rises on Axe Edge above Buxton, has imposed its surface drainage by down-cutting some 650ft/200m through the 350 million-year-old Carboniferous limestone of the White Peak plateau.

To find out how that happened, we have to go back 10,000 years to the end of the last Ice Age, when the area was still blanketed by huge glaciers coming from the north. The alignment of the existing Dove Valley may have guided ice movement and channelled melt-waters during deglaciation, following the sinuous nature of the river valley and cutting through the rock much like a knife does through butter.

But why did some rocks, like the spectacular features of Thorpe Cloud, Bunster Hill, and the prominent pinnacles of Pickering Tor, Ilam Rock and the Twelve Apostles, not get ground down by the icy, rushing melt-water? The answer is that they were made of much harder reef limestone, which formed as coral reefs on the edges of that tropical Carboniferous sea 350 million years ago. The Ice Age meltwater river wound around them, eventually isolating them and forming the upstanding features we see today.

What about the caves, such as Dove Holes, Reynard's Cave and the small one beneath Pickering Tor? Caves often occur within reef limestone, and are usually formed by what is known as lateral stream erosion – that is they have been hollowed out by those same meltwater streams in slightly weaker areas of the limestone.

TOP: Thorpe Cloud

A WALK THROUGH THE DALE

The three-mile walk through the main part of the dale to Milldale starts at the famous **Stepping Stones**, beneath the twin entrance portals of Bunster Hill (on the Staffordshire bank) and Thorpe Cloud, on the Derbyshire side. In Victorian times, you could hire a donkey from a character called 'Donkey Billy' to bring you to the Stepping Stones from Thorpe Station. It's much easier to cross the river now because of the controversial refurbishment of the stones by Derbyshire County Council in 2010.

The stones take you across to the Derbyshire bank and left through a 'dual carriageway' squeezer stile into the water meadows. These are a very popular place for picnicking families during summer months. The weirs in the river were added in Victorian times to impound the water for fish in times of drought.

The first named rock formation is **Dovedale Castle**, a short distance along the river from the Stepping Stones on the Staffordshire bank. A set of steps allegedly built by Italian prisoners of war in the Second World War climbs steadily up to the bare limestone promontory known as **Lover's Leap**.

The story goes that a young woman who believed her lover had been killed in the Napoleonic Wars threw herself off the top of the rocks, but her flapping skirts caught in the branches of a tree as she fell and saved her life. Thankfully, when she got home she heard that her boyfriend was alive and well.

TOP: Stepping Stones
MIDDLE: Lover's Leap
BOTTOM: The Twelve Apostles from across the river

There is a fine view from here of the lower reaches of the dale, and on the opposite side of the Dove sticking up through the trees is a large group of limestone pinnacles called the **Twelve Apostles**. These were created from the harder reef limestone, and the National Trust faces a constant battle to keep the trees from obscuring the rocks.

Steps now lead down to the river again and you soon come to the reef limestone pinnacles of **Tissington Spires** on the right, so named because they mark the boundary of that parish.

On the hillside opposite, the buttress of **Jacob's Ladder** stands proud, and perched on the horizon on the edge of the dale above is the aptly-named **Air Cottage**, which must have one of the finest views in the White Peak.

A few steps further on, the natural arch known as **Reynard's Cave** comes into view, high on the dale side to the right. Formed by differential erosion in the hard reef limestone, the vegetated arch shelters a shallow cave known as **Reynard's Kitchen**.

Now the sheer limestone walls of the dale sides draw in to the section known as **The Straits**, and wooden duckboards take you through an area where flooding is frequent. Tenacious yew trees cling to the vertical sides, and the distinctive profile known as **Lion's Head Rock** can be made out if you look back. Precariously perched on the crags above is the detached rock known as **The Watchbox**.

TOP: Reynard's Cave
MIDDLE: Pickering Tor
BOTTOM: Strolling through Dovedale

As you approach the junction with Hall Dale (on the left), twin spear-like pinnacles of **Pickering Tor** (on the right) and **Ilam Rock** (opposite) rear up from the floor of the dale. The wooden footbridge by Pickering Tor leads up into Hall Dale via Hurt's Wood, but keep to the river-side path which leads east towards the cavernous large water-worn caves known as **Dove Holes**.

Beyond Nab's Dale (on the right), the dale opens out again into pleasant water meadows, frowned down on the opposite bank by the vertical cliff face of **Raven's Tor**. Unfortunately this no longer is the home of the sinister croaking crows.

The easy path now leads on to the tiny hamlet of **Milldale**, which is reached by crossing the narrow packhorse bridge known as **Viator's Bridge**, in reference to its celebrated appearance in *The Compleat Angler*.

A further two miles on from Milldale will take you to **Lode Mill** and past **Peaseland Rocks** and **Drabber Tor** into **Wolfscote Dale** and **Beresford Dale**. In Beresford Dale, you pass **Pike Pool** and the **Fishing Temple,** inscribed to Walton and Cotton, in the grounds of Cotton's former home among the trees across the river. There is no access to the Fishing Temple. Finally a green track leads into **Hartington** past the conical, and supposedly hollow, hill known as **Pennilow** on the right.

ABOVE: Viator's Bridge, Milldale   OPPOSITE: Wolfscote Dale

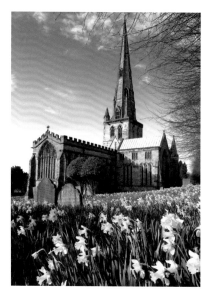

ASHBOURNE AND THE SURROUNDING VILLAGES

Ashbourne

The sign at the entrance to Ashbourne declares that it is the gateway to Dovedale. But it is also one of Derbyshire's finest old towns in its own right, a feast of wonderful Georgian architecture and St Oswald's Parish Church, one of the most impressive and elegant churches in the country.

Most of St Oswald's dates from rebuilding in the 13th century and is principally in the classic Early English style. The tower and the elegant spire, which rises to 212ft (30m), were built between 1330 and 1350 in the Perpendicular style. The alabaster monuments and tombs to the Cokayne and Bradbourne families in the north transept chapel are justly famous, but perhaps the best-known monument is Thomas Banks's moving, white Carrara marble figure of Penelope Boothby, who died in 1791 at the tender age of five.

TOP LEFT: St Oswald's Church Ashbourne TOP RIGHT: Penelope Boothby Monument
BOTTOM RIGHT: Alstonefield

Across Church Street from St Oswald's is the magnificent, mullioned and stone-built Old Grammar School founded in 1585 by Sir Thomas Cokayne on behalf of Elizabeth I. Opposite the Grammar School is the classical Georgian front of The Mansion, built in 1685 for Dr. John Taylor, another friend of Samuel Johnson, who was a regular visitor.

Further down St John Street is a 'gallows' inn sign which crosses the street and advertises two former coaching inns – the Green Man and the Black's Head – now combined into one. St John Street leads up to Ashbourne's sloping, triangular Market Place, where weekly markets have been held since 1296 and today take place every Thursday and Saturday.

ASHBOURNE FOOTBALL

Ashbourne's most famous tradition is the Shrove Tuesday and Ash Wednesday Football Game. This is played through the streets of the town by teams of no set number who represent the 'Up'ards' and the 'Down'ards' respectively – the Henmore Brook being the dividing line. The object of the game is for the Up'ards to score a 'goal' at the wall of Sturston Mill, a mile and a half upstream, or the Down'ards at a stone marking the site of Clifton Mill, a mile and a half in the opposite direction.

Alstonefield

Standing 900 feet (274m) up on a ridge between the Dove and the Manifold, Alstonefield (which includes the hamlet on Milldale) is one of the highest villages in the Peak. Its mullion-windowed cottages cluster around the village green, where markets were held until 1500. Cattle sales were held in the yard of the The George public house on the green, which is a favourite for walkers exploring Dovedale.

Inside the mainly Norman parish church of St Peter's is the elaborate grey-green pew of Charles Cotton's family from nearby Beresford Hall.

Hartington

Hartington, at the northern end of Dovedale, still wears the air of a prosperous market town, although it is nearly 800 years since its market charter was first granted and many years since a market was last held in its spacious Square. The classical three-arched facade of the Town Hall, built in 1836, adds to this urban impression, and The Square is ringed by elegant 18th and 19th century stone cottages.

TOP LEFT: Hartington Hall YHA BOTTOM LEFT: Ilam Church
TOP RIGHT: Mock Gothic Eleanor Cross in Ilam

The Charles Cotton Hotel is a reminder of one of Hartington's most famous sons, co-author with Izaak Walton of *The Compleat Angler*, who lived at Beresford Hall in nearby Beresford Dale. The Hartington Cheese Factory, one of a handful in the country which was licensed to produce Stilton cheese, closed in 2009, and there are plans to redevelop the site for housing. A shop and visitor centre in the village explains the long process involved in producing the famous blue-veined 'King of English cheeses.'

Perhaps the most famous visitor to Hartington was Prince Charles Edward Stuart (Bonnie Prince Charlie) on his ill-fated march on London in 1645. He is alleged to have stayed at the lovely Tudor mansion of Hartington Hall, south-east of the village centre, which is now surely one of the most palatial youth hostels in the country. Hartington Hall was built by Robert Bateman in 1611, and is a typical Derbyshire three-gabled, stone-mullioned manor house.

The hill-top parish church of St Giles is interesting, with a two-storey porch, transepts and aisles dating mainly from the 13th and 14th centuries. The massive battlemented west tower stands watch over the village below. Hartington stands at the centre of one of the biggest parishes in the country, divided into four quarters – Town, Upper, Nether and Middle.

Ilam

Ilam is very much an estate village, largely designed in the *cottage ornee* style by John Shaw for shipping magnate Jesse Watts Russell in the 1830s. The village centre is dominated by the mock-Gothic Eleanor cross, which was erected by Watts Russell in memory of his wife in 1840, and was recently restored by villagers.

The saddleback-towered parish church of the Holy Cross has ancient origins, and contains the tomb of the late Saxon St Bertelin (or Bertram) and has two Saxon or Viking age crosses in its churchyard. The church, over-restored by Gilbert Scott in 1855, also contains the ostentatious mausoleum to Watts Russell's father-in-law, David Pike Watts, and a tomb by Sir Francis Chantry.

Ilam Hall was rebuilt in the Gothic style by Watts Russell in 1828, but was partly demolished in the 1930s. Ilam Park (NT) is set beside the River Manifold, and enjoys outstanding views towards the hills of Dovedale and the Manifold Valley. There is a well-appointed information centre and tea-room.

The Dovedale Sheepdog Trails, now held on August Bank Holiday Monday, have been held at the Blore crossroads in Ilam since 1891.

Tissington

For many visitors, Tissington is the complete White Peak village, especially on Ascension day when the five beautiful well-dressings – traditionally among the first and earliest-recorded in the Peak – are in place. The neat village green is complete with a duck pond, and everything is watched over by the elegant Jacobean manor house of Tissington Hall and the squat Norman tower of the parish church.

Tissington Hall has been the home of the FitzHerbert family for four centuries and several rooms of this charming house are open to the public. From the stone-flagged Main Hall, the visitor is shown the oak-panelled Dining Room, the Library and the East and West Drawing Rooms. The present house dates from the early 18th century, but has been much added to over the centuries.

There is an award-winning tea room in the former coach house close to the hall. On the hillside opposite is the splendid Norman church of St Mary's. Although heavily restored in 1854, there is much Norman work still to be seen inside, including the south doorway, the chancel arch and the original 11th century tub-shaped font.

ABOVE: Tissington well-dressing

THE TISSINGTON TRAIL

Avoiding Tissington in a wide sweep to the east is the Tissington Trail, a pleasant walking and riding route which follows the line of the former Ashbourne to Buxton railway line, closed by Dr Beeching in 1967.

It was one of the last lines to be built during the 'Railway Age', opening in 1894, and was re-opened by the National Park Authority as a leisure route in 1971. You can now hire cycles to ride along it, or just enjoy walking along the traffic-free route which passes through some of the finest of the White Peak's rolling countryside.

FURTHER INFORMATION

Accommodation

Lists of various types of accommodation can be obtained from the Visitor Information Centre in Ashbourne ☎ 01335 343666. There is a full range of serviced accommodation: hotels, guest houses, bed and breakfasts, farm houses, youth hostels, camping and caravan sites.

Tourist Information Centre

Ashbourne Visitor Information Centre
Town Hall, Market Place, Ashbourne, Derbyshire DE6 1EU;
☎ 01335 343666; www.visitpeakdistrict.com

Bakewell Visitor Centre
The Old Market Hall, Bridge Street, Bakewell, Derbyshire DE45 1DS;
☎ 01629 816558; www.peakdistrict.gov.uk

Manifold Valley Visitor Centre, Hulme End, Nr Buxton, Derbyshire SK17 0EZ;
☎ 01298 84679; www.discoverstaffordshirepeakdistrict.com; open seasonally.

There is also an unmanned National Trust Information Point in Milldale.

Toilets

There are public toilets in Ashbourne; at the main car park in Dovedale; Milldale and in Mill Lane, Hartington.

Maps

For walking in and around Dovedale it is recommended that you buy the OS Explorer Map OL24 (1:25,000) The Peak District, White Peak.

Cycle hire

Ashbourne Cycle Hire, Mapleton Lane, Ashbourne, Derbyshire. DE6 2AA; ☎ 01335 343156; www.peakdistrictcycleways.co.uk, see website for details.

Carsington Water Visitor Centre, Ashbourne, Derbyshire; ☎ 01629 540696; www.peakdistrictcycleways.co.uk; see website for details.

Miner's Arms, Main Road, Carsington Village, Derbyshire; ☎ 01629 540207; www.peakdistrictcycleways.co.uk; see website for details.

Manifold Track Cycle Hire Centre, Old Station Car Park, Earlsway, Waterhouses, Staffs.ST10 3EG; ☎ 01538 308609; www.peakdistrictcycleways.co.uk; see website for details.

Published by Bradwell Books
9 Orgreave Close Sheffield S13 9NP
Email – books@bradwellbooks.co.uk

2nd Edition
ISBN – 9781909914094
Print – Gomer Press, Llandysul, Ceredigion SA44 4JL

Design – Andy Caffrey
Typeset – Mark Titterton
Photography – © Mark Titterton
Words – © Roly Smith

FRONT COVER: Twelve Apostles
BACK COVER LEFT Stepping Stones MIDDLE: Reynard's Cave RIGHT: Wolfscote Dale
BOTTOM: Ilam